YOU ARE NOT **DUST**

You Are Created to Be Fire like God

ADOLPHUS UZOAMAKA CYPRIAN

BALBOA.
PRESS

A DIVISION OF HAY HOUSE

Balboa Press books may be ordered through
booksellers or by contacting:

Balboa Press
A Division of Hay House
1663 Liberty Drive
Bloomington, IN 47403
www.balboapress.com
1 (877) 407-4847

Because of the dynamic nature of the Internet, any web addresses or
links contained in this book may have changed since publication and
may no longer be valid. The views expressed in this work are solely those
of the author and do not necessarily reflect the views of the publisher,
and the publisher hereby disclaims any responsibility for them.

The author of this book does not dispense medical advice or prescribe
the use of any technique as a form of treatment for physical, emotional,
or medical problems without the advice of a physician, either directly
or indirectly. The intent of the author is only to offer information
of a general nature to help you in your quest for emotional and
spiritual well-being. In the event you use any of the information in
this book for yourself, which is your constitutional right, the author
and the publisher assume no responsibility for your actions.

Any people depicted in stock imagery provided by Thinkstock are
models, and such images are being used for illustrative purposes only.
Certain stock imagery © Thinkstock.

Print information available on the last page.

ISBN: 978-1-5043-8892-4 (sc)
ISBN: 978-1-5043-8893-1 (e)

Balboa Press rev. date: 10/03/2017

Dedication

To my Lord Jesus Christ.

Contents

Acknowledgement

I wish to say a very big thank you to God Almighty for His Grace. I will also want to appreciate my wife whose impact in my life has been very positive, her contribution towards this book is immeasurable. And to my Father in the Lord; Pastor Mishael Ike Ohiri whose prayers and support have made this book a reality. I will not forget to say a big thank you to my mother and brothers and sisters for their prayers.

I am very grateful to my lecturer; DR. ADEBAYO TUNDE OKUMEDE Dunamis Christian University whose valuable advice helped me in this book, including my kind lecturers at Dunamis Christian University and The Redeemed Bible College.

I will not forget to send my regards to entire staff of Dunamis Christian University, our Vice Chancellor. Rev. Dr. Osibowale and the Chancellor of Dunamis Christian University, Rev Dr. Olorunleye.

Preface

There are two nature in man; The nature of God and nature of Adam. The nature of God is fire and the nature of Adam is dust. When the nature of God dominates a man, the man is said to be born again; this means that the man has received the Holy Spirit and has been converted to fire.

When the nature of Adam dominates a man, the man is said to be a dust, that is, a meal to the devil.

When a man becomes fire, he becomes a direct enemy to the devil. When a man is dust, which is Adamic nature, he becomes direct food to the devil. Whichever way; either fire (An enemy of devil) or dust, (A food for devil).

Genesis 3v19; 'In the sweat of thy face shalt thou eat bread, till thou return unto the ground, for out of it wast thou taken: for dust thou art, and unto dust shalt thou return'

This statement was from the Father to His Son. Actually, the Adamic nature in man is the cause of being a dust. God did not plan to make any man a dust. He said clearly, that man was taken from the ground. Not that man was made with dust. Man was made out of the ground or out of dust not from dust.

Considering some factors such as gold. Gold is made out of the ground. No gold is made without passing it through fire.

Infact, most of the cherished ornaments, jewelries or precious stones are taken out of the ground. They are not made with the dust or sand of the ground but are taken out of it and can only be appreciated and regarded as valuables until they pass through fire. Fire gives them the value they have. So, man was not made with dust particles as we think, rather man was made out of dust like gold. What makes you a man is fire.

Even, the Bible said that God created other animals with His word; "Let there be" statement, but yet when the same animal dies it returns to dust. The same thing happens to man.

The Bible said that the first Adam sinned against God and he lost his position of being a fire and was converted to dust and the last Adam **(Jesus Christ)** became righteous and did not sin and was converted to fire.

What actually makes a man different from other animals is his ability to become fire.

Foreword

The writer of this book made a systematic themetical exegesis of a great and profound analysis, which is essentially based on a well articulated idea in understanding a depth of conceptualization and an essence of expression that is largely dependent on inspirational insight of the Holy Ghost.

The work gives credence to the importance of good theological training for one that is called by God as the writer is my present student at Master level at Dunamis Christian University Lagos, Nigeria. The scriptures rightly said, "Deep calleth unto deep". The scope and depth of one elucidation on any Biblical theme is essentially dependent on the level of exposure that the person has in both knowledge and understanding. It is expedient to note that this work is a proffered solution to the major reasons that impair believers growth today, believers at very high percentage get involved in adultery error called syncretism, based on ignorant of their person inherent.

The theory of man dust and man fire is timely for our contemporary believers are enlightened on their place with that.

A tactful look on the writer's theory of man dust and man fire shall go a long way in correcting the misconception of believers on the strength of Satan power over mankind particularly the believer, which the strength of Satan against man is largely dependent on the level of man being ignorant of himself or herself and that. This work has really come to bridge the ignorant man dust to the place of knowledge man fire, and make man a terror to Satan. I say kudos to the writer. This book is the manual of deliverance that believers are running helter skelter for, thereby getting involved in the error of syncretism in Christendom.

The scriptures made a pertinent statement in Jer: 5v4, it reads thus' "Therefore, I said, surely these are poor, they are foolish for they know not the way of the Lord, nor the judgment of their hand. Had work within these principles, when you lack the knowledge of that principles, you walk in presumption, and presumption can only lead the ignorant mankind to transgression, that make man dust the devil's meat. Hence, I strongly recommend we apply the revelation in this book and leverage it over Satan attack through revelation and become man fire in Christ Jesus.

DR. ADEBAYO TUNDE OKUMEDE
LECTURER, DUNAMS CHRISTIA UNIVERSITY.

CHAPTER ONE

CONSIDER THIS

Imagine this, if you just wake up early one morning, and discover that a group of armed men has surrounded your house, broken your door, bundled you out of your bed, and asked you to denounce Christ or else, they will kill you; what will you do?

This is a very serious issue based on the type of Christianity we practice these days. It is assumed that in the modern day, Christianity is growing cold. There is no more fire in our Christian life. This is very dangerous in this our ungodly generation.

If you look at the life of the early Christians, the way they were killed and their general attitude towards Christianity, you will discover that there is one ingredient missing in the life of the present day Christians. The present day Christianity has become a bread, butter and tea party. Churches and fellowships, "come as you are" syndrome is eating deep into our churches and this is very bad, because it is satanic lie that quenches the fire in Christians.

Let us take a look at some of the early Christian martyrs and see how they overcame the tribulations they suffered. First of all, let us look at the life of Peter, one of the greatest Apostles, the first Christian leader, and the most outspoken of all the twelve Apostles. He denied Christ when he was still living in the flesh. Peter said to Jesus;

> **'Though all men shall be offended because of thee, yet will I never be offended'. (offended: ie, though the faith of other men should be shaken and fail, yet mine will be firm and constant). Jesus said to him, 'Verily I say unto thee, this night, before the cock crow, thou shalt deny me thrice'. Peter said to him, 'Though I should die with thee, yet will I not deny thee." Likewise also said all the disciples.**

> **Now Peter sat without in the palace: and a damsel came unto him, saying, Thou also wast with Jesus of Galilee. But he denied before them all, saying, I know not what thou sayest. And when he was gone out into the porch, another maid saw him, and said unto them that were there, "This fellow was also with Jesus of Nazareth." And again he denied with an oath, "I do not know the man." And after a while came unto him they that stood by, and said to Peter, "Surely thou also art one of them; for thy speech bewrayeth thee." And Peter remembered the words of Jesus, which said unto him, "Before the cock crow, thou shalt deny me thrice." And he went out, and wept bitterly. (Matthew 26v33-35,69-75).**

But when the fire of Pentecost came upon him; the same Peter became as bold as a lion, converting, at a single blow, 3,000 souls to Christ **(Act 2v 14 - 42).** He was martyred as a very brave man.

Let's see how some of the Apostles were murdered;

Historically tradition tells us that Peter was executed under the reign of Emperor Nero. He was crucified upside down, at his own request because he did not consider himself worthy to be crucified in the same manner that the Lord Jesus was crucified. Paul, who spear-headed the martyrdom of Stephen, after he caught the fire of revival on his way to Damascus, wrote most of the epistles. He did so many remarkable works for Christ. He was beheaded with the sword in Rome, about the same time that Peter was killed.

Stephen, the first Christian martyr, caught the fire and became bold to talk to the Jewish Council **(Act 6v5-9, Act 7v59).** He was stoned to death and the bible recorded that he bravely accepted his fate.

The first 300 years of the church which were commonly known as the **HEROIC AGE OF THE CHURCH,** was the time when the church went through the greatest persecution yet the church grew more. The first Emperor to persecute the Christians was Nero. In the year 64 A.D; during his reign, fire broke out in Rome for six days and nights that the fire burned, the greater part of the city was laid in ruin.

The rumour later spread that Nero himself had caused the city to be set on fire. This caused the people of Rome to develop great hatred for the emperor. To salvage his battered image, Nero accused the Christians of having set fire on Rome. The accusation certainly was not true, but large numbers of Christians were arrested and a terrible persecution followed.

Many Christians were even crucified. Some were sown up in the skins of wild beasts, then big lions were let loose against them, and they were torn to pieces. Women were tied to mad bulls and dragged until they died. After night fall, Christians were burnt at the stake inside Nero's garden.

The Roman people who hated Christians were free to come into the garden, and Nero drove wickedly around in his chariot, enjoying the horrible scene. The martyrs that died during this period of time were called the **Neronian Martyrs,** or the **Protomartyrs of Rome.** They were honoured at the site in Vatican City called the **Piazza of the Protomartyrs.**

How did the early Christians deal with the matter? Did they come together to form an army so that they could fight back? Did they turn away from the Christian faith because it cost so much to be a believer? No, the Christians absorbed cruelty with courage and they absorbed hatred with heroism and conquered fierceness with faith.

They withstood the persecution because they had fire in them. You can call it fire of revival or fire of the Holy Ghost. It was the fire that kept them through even unto death.

Another great example among the martyrs was Polycarp, a man who lived in the second century A.D. He was arrested and brought into the great amphitheater in Smyrna (in Asia Minor).

Thousands of people were there to watch what would happen. The ruler reminded Polycarp of his great age and he urged him to deny his Christian faith; **"Denounce Christ and I will release you"** But Polycarp said; **"Eighty and six years have I served him, and he has never done me wrong; how can I blaspheme Him, my King who has saved me? I am a Christian (He shouted)"**

The ruler then cried out to the crowd; **"Polycarp has confessed himself to be a Christian"** The crowds yelled; **"Let him be burned".** Wood was collected and made into a pile. Polycarp asked not to be fastened to the stake.

He said; **"Leave me thus, he who strengthen me to endure the flames will also enable me to stand firm at the stake without being fastened with nails"** As the piled wood was lighted, Polycarp bravely lifted up a final prayer to his God and the flame consumed him. He died in 156 A.D.

Another man who died in these early years of the church was named JUSTIN. He was whipped and beheaded in

Rome about 165 A.D. His last words were these; **"We desire nothing more than to suffer for our Lord Jesus Christ"**. He was known as **JUSTIN MARTYR.**

After the first 300 years of church history, a change took place; Christianity became the official religion of the Roman Empire. Christianity became a popular religion and Christians were no longer persecuted. It was also during this less turbulent time that the church became more and more worldly and corrupt. That is, the fire began to die in the life of believers due to lackadaisical attitude of Christians.

One thing about fire is that it has a very easy way of spreading around, most especially, where there were dry grasses and light papers. The moment they kill one of the Christian, up to 100 people around catch the fire.

When they killed Jesus Christ, he ascended because he is a fire, 120 disciples caught the fire. When Peter addressed the crowd, 3000 people caught the fire and in another meeting 5000 people caught the fire. The fire kept on spreading with little effort from the disciples.

So, the disciples were set on fire and thousands of people that came to watch them were like dry grasses and light papers; the moment the disciples were killed, the dry grasses and light papers around caught the fire and kept on burning. The more they were killed, the more Christianity spread.

In our modern day Christianity, it looks as if the only person that has the fire is usually the founder of a ministry or the general overseer of a church. In this regard, the General overseer becomes fire and every other person becomes pot.

When you place a pot on top of fire, the pot catches fire, in as much as the pot is still on the fire, it will keep on burning more and more. The moment the pot is taken out of fire, the pot gradually gets cold until it becomes ice cold.

Fire is an essential ingredient that got missing in

our modern Christian life. People are no longer striving to becoming fire; rather, people are looking for instant miracles. They want to follow a person that has the fire but never wanted to have the fire themselves.

The bible tells us that the Spirit of God in us always makes us become bold with a sound mind **(2Timothy 1v7).**

Look at Justin, the Martyr. An apologist of the faith, confronted one of the Leaders in the Roman Empire, called Marcion who rejected the Old Testament and issued his own new testament which consisted part of the gospel of Luke and 10 of Paul's epistles only. Justin was so bold to write a defence of Christianity concerning that and addressed the letter to Emperor Augustus Caesar. He wrote; **"You can kill us but you cannot hurt us".**

The early Christians always fixed their minds on the words of Christ **(John 15 & 16).**

These words of Christ were like courage to them, they were able to despise worldly tortures and purchased eternal life with their enduring spirit. To them, the fire of their cruel torturers was cold, but they kept on remembering and fixing their eyes on how they have escaped from the eternal and unquenchable fire of hell

Christians are salt and light in a corrupted world. We are to influence the world and not the world influencing us. We are to stand against and hold back the corrupting influence of sin and sinners who want to influence others, especially the young ones.

We are in the world but separated for service to Christ. When we stand up for righteousness that is found in Christ and God's word, we should expect people to be against us; but really, they are not against us, but God's standard and principles.

We cannot influence the corrupt world if we are cold. If we do not have fire to burn the dry grasses and light papers around us, we automatically become dry grasses and light papers.

Despite all the Christian programmes on TV and internet today, we are left hardly knowing the truth. Many want to Christianize the world by flesh and not by fire and it probably will not be long before we make the same mistake of abandoning the power of the gospel and showing the light of Christ in us and instead want to use force to convert others.

Any religion that uses force to convert others shows that it is weak in convincing people that it has something from God. Using force to enforce one's religion proves that you do not represent the true God. You do not use force to convert people to Christianity rather through signs and wonders.

There is no way you can perform signs and wonders if you are not a fire. We are practicing Christianity of flesh and not Christianity of the spirit. For Christianity of the spirit is in the fire of the Holy Ghost.

You must be a fire to practice true Christianity in this our modern world because persecution can come in different ways at any time. If you do not possess the fire, you are likely to denounce Christ.

Look at this; a man preaching in a public bus was vibrating, quoting the bible from Genesis to Revelation like a true believer, without knowing that there were armed robbers in the bus. One of the robbers brought out a gun and point at the man and said; **"If you don't drop that bible, I will shoot you"**. The man, being flesh, began to beg. As the pressure became stronger, he dropped the bible, unfortunately, they shot him and he died after dropping the bible. Persecution comes at anytime, anywhere and in different form. If you are not fire even if you quote the bible from beginning to the end, you will likely denounce Christ, like the preacher, when such situation comes your way.

So, fire is the essential ingredient that makes you withstand all odd time and face any fierce persecution without denying Christ as your Lord. Today, be a fire and excel.

CHAPTER TWO

IN THE BEGINNING

There is an important ingredient missing in the life of Christians today. This missing ingredient is fire. God created you to be a fire like Him. The bible said that God created us in His own image and likeness. He is fire; so, we should be fire like our God.

In the book of Genesis, the way, purpose and method through which God created man was clearly stated. It was discovered that God created man with his hands. In creating other animals, he made a pronouncement.

That is, "Let there be" statement. In creating man, he molded man with His hands after declaring, 'Let us make man in our own image and likeness' **(Genesis 1:26)**

In Genesis 2v7, consider this statement:

> **'Then the Lord God formed man out of the dust from the ground and breathed the breath of life into his nostrils and the man become a living being'**

If you look at it critically, you will discover that you do not mold dust. Dust is made to fly around in the air, it is a useless part of sand. In the book of **Psalm 18v42.**

'Then I beat them as fine as the dust before the wind. I cast them out like dirt in the street'.

Dust is a particle of sand that is not useful, normally carried away by the wind. In **Psalm 18v42**, the Psalmist was talking about how he turned his adversaries into dust that the wind carried away.

Dust cannot be molded. but carried around by the wind.

Let's also consider the parable of the Potter in **Jeremiah 18 v 6B,**

'Just like clay in the Potters hand, so are you in my hand, house of Israel'.

Here, God Himself, not Moses, really showed the real insight of his secret of molding man.

As Potters use clay to mold pot, and other utensils, so, God used clay to mold man. The bible said that after he had finished molding man, he breathed into man's nostril. To be sure, God make man in likeness to the way a potter molds the pot.

That is, after a potter completes the molding process, he refines the pot. Ok, refining is the process of heating the pot with enough fire to make it ready for use.

In fact, I grew up in a village where there were many potters. Whenever they finished making a pot, they would keep it and at the final stage, they gather the whole pot and set a fierce fire on them.

Some of the pots usually break as a result of the intense heat. Fire will heat the pots for some moment until they become red. Anyone that appears red and does not break is removed from the fire, until all are removed.

The parable of the potter is likened to the creation of man. In other word, God heated man with his fire to actually become like him as he planned. God did not just create man and breathe into man. He followed the principle of the potter. That is, after making man, he refined man with fire to make him the real image of God.

What are those attributes of God in man that make man a real image of God?

1. Self-willed
2. Creative ability
3. Possession of power to control
4. Ability to live forever

SELF-WILLED

Self-will is an attribute of God in a man which allows a man to make a personal decision without being influenced by the Spirit of God or another man.

God said;

'I have created the good and the bad; I have created life and death chose life that you may live (Deuteronomy 30v19).

He also said,

'I wish above all things that you may prosper and be of good health" (3John 1v2).

All those things God mentioned are good, but, it is a matter of choice. Someone can decide to choose doing evil; God can only warn the person to stop doing that. The person may decide to stop or continue. Whatever he chooses is his will.

When Christ was about to be crucified, terrible fear came on him. He has the will to say, I am no more dying again or say, let me just die. But he prayed, father, not my will but your will **(Luke 22v42).** No wonder when he was teaching his disciples how to pray, he never forgot to tell them to always ask for the will of God in their lives **(Matthew 6v10).**

Look at the lives of the martyred Christians, at a point, many began to give themselves willingly to be martyred. It was out of their own free will that most of the martyrs were killed. They have right to denounce Christ and live.

As a man, you have every right to ask for God's will in your life and you have every right to do things in your own way. However, you cannot choose the consequences of your decision.

When Adam sinned, God knows that Adam has the right to eat or not to eat the fruit; he ate not because his wife persuaded him. It was his choice to accept or reject.

Eve never forced Adam to eat. Even when he said that it was the woman that deceived him, God did not pay attention to him because God knows that, he would have reported her to Him (God) if she tried to force him. He ate the fruit out of his will.

Whatever a man does in life is out of his will. The gospel is preached to you; you can accept it or reject it. It is your will. Just control your will-power and always remember that every decision has an out-come.

The outcome of every decision is not controlled by man's will. In this regard, man needs to be very careful of his decision. Like our Lord, Christ Jesus, we must not forget to ask for the will of God. In many cases, His will always contradicts our will. That is, it comes as an opposite to our will.

Before Satan makes you to sin, he first works on your will-power. Satan did not force Eve to eat the fruit. He only knew that Eve had been lusting after the fruit. The way she glanced and stared at those beautiful and appetizing fruits and imagined how they would taste.

Then she pondered, **"But, why did God ask my husband**

not to eat this fruit?" She now saw Satan as the person that had the answer to her question.

"Did God say you should not eat of this fruit?" that is the question Satan threw at her. Her response revealed that she had already made up her mind long before Satan came. Her answer sounds like this, **'I wanted to eat, but God said we should not eat and the fruit look sweet'.**
Gen. 3 v 2-3:

> **The woman said to the serpent, "We may eat the fruit from the trees in the garden, but about the fruit of the tree in the middle of the garden, God said, 'you must not eat it or touch it or you will die".**

Ok, look at that; when she was talking of other fruits God gave them permission to eat, she did not say God said, we should eat, but when she wanted to talk about the one God asked them not to eat, she used the word God said; obviously she had made up her mind long before that time else, she would not have fallen. The bible called Satan, the deceiver.

It means he does not have power over you. However he is subtle in nature. He comes to fine-tune your will and makes you say or do something against God's will.

CREATIVE ABILITY

> **God said let there be light and there was light. (Genesis 1V3).**

In creativity, God is the best. He said;

> **let us make man in our image and likeness- (Genesis 1v26).**

12

Looking at it from the creative angle, you will discover that God does not joke with creativity. This explains why God hates idolatry so much.

He knows that man can create images that look like angels and even himself. Man's creative ability has helped to reshape the world. Look around: the plane flying in the sky, the cars of all sorts, the ship in the sea, the buildings, and the rocket that enters the moon, the internet and roads...

If you critically look at those things, you will discover that God's gift to humanity is so rich that man deserves not to fail in life.

As a man is born, he inherits the ability to create. Look at the world of literature, music, dance, and movie. All these things are God-like character in man.

Man has the ability to imagine a thing and his imagination becomes real; so man inherited creativity from God.

POSSESSION OF POWER TO CONTROL.

God said;

'Let him have dominion over the birds of the air; (Genesis 1v28).

Among the three reasons why man seek any god or God is 'power', of course, there are three 'Ps' which are the basic reasons man seeks to worship a God.

They are;
1. Power
2. Protection
3. Provision

Man often seeks for power, protection and provision from any God. That is the reason man will leave one god and begin to seek after another god.

If any man feels that he is not secured with the god he

serves in the area of power, protection and provision, he looks for another god. If any man feels that the god he is serving is too harsh, he looks for another god.

Little did man know that the power he is chasing after was given to him right from the beginning of creation. **The fact that man became captive to Satan, did not take away the position of man from the earth.**

The power to dominate is still with him. Little did he know that Satan is just using the will-power of man to intimidate man and subject man to serve him.

The power that we seek as men is in us and nothing takes it away from us other than ignorance. Even God gave us dominion over dangerous animals such as snakes, scorpions, lions etc.

We run away from demons (evil) spirits without knowing that the major reason why they often succeded in attacking us is fear. They know that by creation, you are greater than them.

All they do is to create fear in you by giving you a false message, cage you and turn you into a dwelling place, as well as an agent to win other people.

Fear is the greatest threat existing against man. It is at this period that, man ask God, **'Where are you?'** It is the same fear that makes a man to leave the Almighty God and hook up with a carved image.

God gave man power over all he is afraid of since creation. Man possessed power as god, because as an image of God, he inherited power from God to work as god to other created animals and things.

ABILITY TO LIVE FOREVER.

As God has the ability to live forever, so man has. Man was not created to die.

Man was created to move from one stage of transformation

to another until he becomes a perfect being and become very much like God.

Food is made by God to nourish the body and also serve as a medicine to the body and soul. Judging it from the angle of food, you will discover that though food serves as a means of nourishing our body, it also helps our body to grow old and decay.

Out of the three kinds of tree in the garden, God told Adam not to eat one, especially the one in the middle but Adam did not bother to ask why.

Even, we that are alive never bother to ask why. First, consider the tree: Its fruit will make you strong, grow and nourish your body. Second, its fruit makes your body weak and make you die at a particular time (don't eat it). The fruit of the tree also makes you wise like a witch so that you work against your Creator. Avoid it. The third one makes you strong, grow and nourish you; it will also act as a medicine to you and will help you to be transformed from one level to another until you become perfect being without dying.

God said, we are His image, it means we have the power to live forever, because living forever is one of the attributes of God in man that man lost when Satan caused him to sin against God.

CHAPTER THREE

THE FALL OF MAN

When you read the account of Adam as the first man on earth, you will discover one synonymous thing. Everything on earth was placed under his control.

The bible said whatever he calls a thing, that thing bears the name for life. Let us assume a lion is called a goat.

Do you know that the rumour of a lion around the corner can make a man to leave that environment? Let's assume that the same man hears a rumour of a goat around the corner, do you think the man will run away?

Ok, if the rumour monger calls goat in place of a lion, do you imagine anybody running away? Can you imagine? The name Adam gave to things and animals became what made man to be afraid most of the time. If a lion is called a goat, I think nobody will be afraid of a lion. If a goat is called a lion, I think nobody wants to go near the goat.

The same principle applies after God created man. The Angles believe that God will give them power or charge over man, but he did not. He loved man so much that he called him **ADAM (ADORABLE, DOMINATING ANGELIC MAN).** Most of the Angels frowned at that name. The major reason is that they knew the implication of that name. Some of them murmured, some grumbled.

Then the head of all angles as at that time became so angry that he planned to overthrow God. He gathered other angry angels and convinced them to stand by his side to war against God.

You know, any soldier planning a coup will first gather other soldiers around him to support and fight for him. That was what that angel did. When he was able to convince some angels, he set his target on man.

He did a very good study of man and discovered that man loved God so much and there is no way he could approach man direct. Long ago, man has made up his mind not to eat that forbidding fruit and no one can convince him to do so, except his wife. Satan knew that, Satan also knew that from the beginning, woman owns the home. **(That means any man that wants to live and enjoys his home should give his wife charge over the home).**

From the description, in those days, the serpent was one of the most beautiful animals and is very friendly to man. Satan decided to use the serpent to convince man to eat the fruit. The serpent came and met Eve instead of Adam. The serpent, being a crafty animal, did not ask the woman to eat the fruit, rather, he asked a question that the answer was hidden in a question or questions.

Did God say you should not eat from this tree? (Genesis 3v1).

Eve said Yes, God said out of the other tree we may eat, but of this, we should not".

You see, at times, they accuse Africans for using question to answer question. If you look critically at that, you will discover that so many questions that our Lord Jesus Christ answered to the Jews were questions in return.

17

'Of whose authority do you cast out demons?' Answer: "Of what authority do your children cast out demons?"

Often times, it is a very good practice, most especially when you are dealing with an enemy. One significant thing about a question is that it exposes the content of the heart. This means that if you want to know the content of someone's heart, ask a question.

Simple question, great result. **'Did God say you should not eat from this tree?"** The truth remains that all power was given to man including will-power. No demon or Satan can ever come to you without first of all arresting your will-power. I can tell you that it is out of will that man sins against God. Most sins for example, comes into man's heart in the form of thought. Some come in form of sight, all are from man's will-power.

Let's look closely at this accusation; 'A woman accused a man of using charm on her to make her commit adultery or similar sin. Yes, it is possible, but if you look at that accusation very well, you will discover that the woman in question has long ago given the man room for such act either by her dressing, speaking, demands or conduct. Now, she has developed such interest in her heart, but only trying to resist it because of her marriage. You will discover that the charm works because it has first arrested her will-power and willingly, she goes to the man, and removes her cloths.

Satan used Eve's will-power to make her eat the fruit. The truth remains there before the coming of the serpent, Eve has been lusting after that fruit, because it was very beautiful and appealing to the eyes. She often ask her husband why should God say so? She would go, touch the fruit and even kiss the fruit. I believe, Satan was around at a time when she was kissing the fruit. If you look at it from the description, you will discover that the serpent was on top of the tree that bears the forbidding fruit and Eve was around the there too.

The serpent saw how she touch and kissed the fruit, so he threw the question at her; **'Did God said you should not eat this fruit?'** Often times, when the enemy wants to catch a man, he waits for the man at the cross-road of decision.

Do I do this or should I leave it? Cross-road of decision. When such time comes, let's seek God seriously, because that is what the enemy is waiting for. Eve touched the fruit; the serpent watched her, and asked her a question. **'Did God say you should not eat the fruit?** That means, Eve was at the base of the tree that bears the fruit. Supposing he said; 'did God say you should not eat any of those fruits?' It would be clear that both of them were far from the tree.

That question required a question in return not an answer. Whenever your enemy is asking you a question, digest the question and know if it needs an answer in the form of a question. It is always advisable to use a question to answer an enemy.

'Did God ask you not to eat any of these fruits? (Question). Did I tell you that I am hungry? What is your concern? Did God send you to me? Were you not around when he said so? (Answers)

The serpent would have gone back to his base, but Eve's answer gave room to her fall. It gave room to further explanation. If you have ever seen or been a victim of the fraudsters, they always come to bring to you what you need much and always present them in the form of question, just to arrest your will-power.

Eve failed. That is not the issue When Eve gave her husband the fruit to eat, the bible did not record if Adam protested against his wife's action or not. All we were told was that Eve gave him the fruit and he ate. From further study, it was learnt that Adam was right there with Eve.

Some writers argued that Adam was away and when

he came back, Eve (the wife) gave him the fruit and he ate without asking a question. But from Bible account, we discovered that he was right there listening to the conversation between the serpent and Eve but he never thought of reprimanding Eve, rather, he concurred with her. Let's look at **Genesis 3v6**

> **"Then the woman saw that the tree was good for food and delightful to look at, and that it was desirable for obtaining wisdom, so she took some of its fruit and ate it, she also gave some to her husband who was with her, and he ate it".**

What a mess? Man, why are you falling? Broken marriages, here and there. Unhappy homes, everywhere. Unfulfilled destinies, looming. Immoral activities, robbery, drunkenness, all these came as a result of man obeying woman without reservation. If you have a wife, as a man and you want to enjoy your life, obey her. Otherwise, she will destroy you. The woman that serves your food, washes your cloth, sweeps your home and takes care of your children has a portion of your life with her.

The woman that sleeps with you on the bed, has sexual relationship with you has a portion of your life with her. Be careful.

Adam was not careful at all. Can you imagine, you are at home, a visitor comes looking for your wife and it never occurs to you to ask a question.

Adam's fall was as a result of two major things.

1. He was carried away by the beauty of his wife. The bible described her as the most beautiful thing God ever created, She was called EVE (Full of praise). She was so beautiful to the extent that Satan and other rebellious angels paused and shook their heads and vowed to take her away from her husband. I guess,

Satan started by praising her beauty and all of a sudden, her head swelled and he introduced the topic of eating the forbidden fruit. Adam never wanted to offend her because he never wanted her to be angry. The beauty of Eve became an issue in heaven to the level that angels began to fall.

2. Adam took his position for granted. When man refuses to take his responsibility as a man in the house, the woman takes the position of a man. It is common thing for a man to welcome visitors at home. Imagine Adam and Eve were together when a stranger came, the man left the woman to entertain the stranger. The responsibility of keeping God's commandment is placed on a man. Man enforces that on his family. That is, man makes sure that his family keeps God's commandment. God gave Adam the instruction, Adam passed it to Eve. What is Eve's business to explain the situation to Satan when the husband is there? It would have been easier for Adam to face Satan. **'I do not know, ask my husband, he is here'** would have been her answer. Adam took his position for granted; he did not pick up his responsibility, he pretended not to hear the conversation between Satan and Eve.

CHAPTER FOUR

MAN AS FOOD FOR SATAN

After creating man, God gave specific instructions to man. The instructions included the kinds of food man needs to eat, the kinds of meat man needs to eat. In this regard, it was obvious that certain animals are not made for food for man, most especially, the animals that shew cud without cloven hooves or with cloven hooves but do not shew cud. **Leviticus 11v1-23.**

That means that some animals or meats man eats may become a sin to man. No wonder when the vision of rise, kill and eat came up to Peter, he rejected it. **Act 10v13-15**

Today, because of that vision, people have concluded that God has sanctified all animals for food for man. If that is true, it will show that man has authority to kill and eat any kind of animal be it reptile, fish, mammal etc. provided it is not a human being (cannibalism).

If you look closely, you will discover the implication of the fall of man to Satan. Examine what God said to Satan after the fall of man **(Genesis 3v14-19):**

> **And the LORD God said unto the serpent, Because thou hast done this, thou art cursed above all cattle, and above every beast of the field; upon thy belly shalt thou**

**go, and dust shalt thou eat all the days
of thy life: And I will put enmity between
thee and the woman, and between thy seed
and her seed; it shall bruise thy head, and
thou shalt bruise his heel.**

**Unto the woman he said, I will greatly
multiply thy sorrow and thy conception;
in sorrow thou shalt bring forth children;
and thy desire shall be to thy husband,
and he shall rule over thee. {to thy...: or,
subject to thy husband. And unto Adam he
said, Because thou hast hearkened unto
the voice of thy wife, and hast eaten of the
tree, of which I commanded thee, saying,
Thou shalt not eat of it: cursed is the
ground for thy sake; in sorrow shalt thou
eat of it all the days of thy life; Thorns also
and thistles shall it bring forth to thee;
and thou shalt eat the herb of the field. In
the sweat of thy face shalt thou eat bread,
till thou return unto the ground; for out of
it wast thou taken: for dust thou art, and
unto dust shalt thou return'.**

God said to Satan, **"Because of what you have done
from this day and forever your food will no longer be
the food of Angels rather you will feed on dust"**.

If you read verse 19 of that chapter, you will discover
that God called man dust. He said you shall return to the
ground for you are dust.

Look at the implication, Satan, you will feed on dust,
man you are dust. In other words, it is the legitimate right
of Satan or legal right of Satan to feed on man as man has
legal right to feed on any animal.

So, often times, when we hear about blood sucking

demons, we should not be afraid because it is their right. That makes me to pause and ponder about the plane crash, motor accidents, wars, political unrest, manufacturing of sophisticated weapons, earthquakes, tornados, hurricanes and the likes.

When I begin to wonder how an individual will wake up and offer his fellow human being to an idol without regret, how four university students were murdered, bombing of churches and so on. I begin to see reasons why, even, at the immense wisdom of men, they could not combat terrorism and killings. Why? This is because, these are avenues for Satan to eat up human being.

There are three major different ways through which Satan eats up human beings:

1. By seizing man's destiny or glory
2. By sucking man's blood
3. By eating man's flesh

SEIZING MAN'S DESTINY OR GLORY

The bible makes me to understand that after the fall of Lucifer, he was chased out of Heaven by Arch Angel Michael **(Revelation 12v7).**

All the glory that made him Lucifer was taken away from him and he was driven out of heaven.

From the study, it was discovered that Lucifer means bringer of light. If you read the account of what Lucifer was made up of, you will marvel **(Ezekiel 28v12-15).**

'Son of man, take up a lamentation upon the king of Tyrus, and say unto him, Thus saith the Lord GOD; Thou sealest up the sum, full of wisdom, and perfect in beauty. Thou hast been in Eden the garden of God; every precious stone was thy covering, the sardius, topaz, and the diamond, the beryl,

24

the onyx, and the jasper, the sapphire, the emerald, and the carbuncle, and gold: the workmanship of thy tabrets and of thy pipes was prepared in thee in the day that thou wast created. {sardius: or, ruby}{beryl: or, chrysolite}{emerald: or, chrysoprase. Thou art the anointed cherub that covereth; and I have set thee so: thou wast upon the holy mountain of God; thou hast walked up and down in the midst of the stones of fire. Thou wast perfect in thy ways from the day that thou wast created, till iniquity was found in thee'.

All those glory was taken away from him. (Isaiah 14v12-15); 'How art thou fallen from heaven, O Lucifer, son of the morning! how art thou cut down to the ground, which didst weaken the nations! {O Lucifer: or, O day star}

For thou hast said in thine heart, I will ascend into heaven, I will exalt my throne above the stars of God: I will sit also upon the mount of the congregation, in the sides of the north: I will ascend above the heights of the clouds; I will be like the most High. Yet thou shalt be brought down to hell, to the sides of the pit.

When I was ignorant of this, I used to join the band of people that say; **"God should have collected all the power he gave to Satan".**

God never left any glory to Satan, but the fact remains that Satan, as an ex-angel will live forever. All Satan is living on belongs to man. He seizes the glory of man to survive.

The glory Satan carries about today is the glory he snatched from men. Ignorantly, men give their glory to Satan without knowing.

All the wealth he parades about is the one he snatched from men. Consider the account of how Satan tempted Christ. During one of those temptations, he took Christ to the top of the mountain and showed him the city of men.

He said; 'If you bow down and worship me. I will give these entire cities to you. (Matthew 4v8-9)

The cities he was talking about were built, and owned by men. He has nothing. He is like the proverbial bat. He hangs in the air. He is not accepted in heaven, he is not accepted on earth.

He only comes to fool men on earth and collect their glory and their wealth on which he lives on. Since he was driven out of heaven to hang in the air, he was given nothing except the power to feed on dust, which is man on earth.

SUCKING MAN'S BLOOD

One of the fundamental powers of satanic existence is man's blood, where lies the soul of a man. A man without blood is dead for there lies the glory of a man. A man without blood has lost his glory. Satan hunts for the blood of men like men hunt for water to drink.

Satan can pay any amount of money in any denomination (be it dollar, pounds, naira name it) on earth just to get a cup of blood.

No wonder people that give their life to him often lose such in a very short time. Some Satan followers can give the blood of their loved ones (mother, father, wife, children) to Satan consciously or unconsciously, and get any amount of money in return.

Blood is so precious. Blood makes a man. Blood is life. It is in blood lies the issues of life. Blood is thicker than water. Blood unites.

Satanists often have blood bank. They make sure that it is always filled up. No wonder, on earth today, violence never ceases. Wars, plane crashes, accidents and other ways through which Satanic agents suck human blood never ends. All these will not stop until Christ comes.

Satanists depend on human blood to survive. All that go to him always drink from the same cup of blood with him in order to become one with him.

So, it is true that Satanists roam about with spiritual pipes and funnels seeking for dust that they can drain their blood.

We use to say; 'God, why will you fold your arms and see all these things Satanists are doing to your children and keep quiet?' truly, God sees them but never keeps quiet.

The fact remains that as long as you are dust, Satan has the right to suck your blood without God asking him any question because God has already given dust to Satan as food. Although God is not an author of confusion.

EATING MAN'S FLESH

When I discovered that till today, cannibals still exist, even among the top personalities of the world order, I became afraid. Someone once told me about how he went to see a Satanist and on getting there, the man brought out human heart that was dried, cut it, gave him some and ate the rest. I became afraid, but, I encouraged myself.

Human eaters are on the increase. Those people are Satanic. They are being initiated into it by Satanists. Eating man meat is never a sin to Satan, because it was given to him to eat by God Almighty. **'Dust you shall feed' 'You**

are dust'. Satan has right to eat any part of human flesh as food.

Do not be surprise when you hear that most people that go to Satan or Satanic cult are asked to bring either their child, wife, mother or loved ones, so that they will bake the flesh of such in their oven and share the meat. In return, the fellow will be given whatever he ask for.

The flesh of a man is meat to Satan. There are things that will happen to man on earth that man will begin to ask; **'God why?'** Know it, there is no need to ask God why. Ask yourself who am I? When you get the answer, you will not need to ask God why again.

CHAPTER FIVE

WHY YOU MUST BECOME FIRE

There are two major types of people living on earth; the dust and the fire. Everybody born on the surface of the earth is dust, whether you know it or not. For **Genesis 3v14-19,** makes us to understand that. For all men are dust, consciously or unconsciously.

Dust is the food for the enemy called Satan. This implies that all men are food for Satan. In this context, it means that Satan has the right to feed on the people called dust.

The other kind of people is the fire type. These are people that are made up of fire particles. These people become terror to Satan rather than food.

Which one are you? Dust or Fire? Are you dust or fire? This question can be answered with the most common phrase in the Christian religious faith called 'Born again'

"Born again" is a very common phrase as long as Christianity is concerned. In the book of **John 3v3;**

> **'Verily, verily, I said unto you except a man be born again, he cannot see the kingdom of God".**

This issue of **"born again"** has been explained in different ways by different people. Some say it is all about baptism, some say it is all about giving your life to Christ.

From this phrase, we see two words that hold the entire Christian faith; "Born again"!

Literally, to be born again means that someone was born and needs to be re-born. That is what the bible called re-birth or new-birth. In the book of **1Corinthians 5V17, it is explained that when one is "born again" he is a new creature; old things are passed away and behold all things are made new.**

"Born" means to give birth to a new baby. To give birth to a child, it takes the conjugal relationship of a man and a woman. I want to tell you that once a child is born, the child becomes a dust. It takes the mercy of God to keep such child out of the pew of Satan.

Watch it very well, once a child is born, the Satanists know the destiny of the child, and they definitely come against the destiny of that child. Take a look at the birth of Christ.

The star appeared, the wise men followed the star. Herod saw the star. Satanists always rise against a new born baby, because as a new born baby, he is a dust that is authorized by God for Satan to feed on.

Satan shall snatch the talent, destiny and glory of the child, if the parents of the child are ignorant.

When Christ was born, the angel told the parents to take him away so that the enemy would not snatch his destiny. Many children died for that reason.

To explain more on being born again, you will discover that when a child is born, the child is a dust and when a child is born again, the child becomes fire. So, born again simply means; **'conversion of a soul from dust to fire'.** This is what the bible calls re-birth (spiritual re-birth).

Jesus told Nicodemus that except a man is born again, he remains a dust and a dust remains food for Satan, and such cannot enter the Kingdom of God.

Except a man is born of fire and the Holy Spirit, he remains a dust. Born again is not just giving your life to Christ. It is all about accepting the life of Christ.

It is Christ that gives his life to us. Given your life to Christ is an under-statement. It should be accepting the life of Christ that he gave to us on the cross of Calvary.

When you are born again, you become a fire, when you become a fire, you become a terror to Satan. One converted Satanist confessed that when they went out to carry out an operation of sucking people's blood, they saw two kinds of people. Ones that carried fire on their heads or even, around them, and others without fire at all.

According to him, no matter how small the fire is, they cannot go near such people.

So, if you are a fire, you remain a terror to Satan; if you are a dust, you remain food for Satan.

To become a fire, you must be born again. To be born again, there are principles:
1. Answer the altar call (Give your life to Christ)
2. Under go thorough believers /Baptismal training
3. Laying of hands on the fellow/Baptism
4. Continuous fellowshipping with other believers and constant study of the word, listen to messages from trusted sources
5. Spiritual growth
6. Bursting in to fire

ANSWER ALTER CALL

This is the first step to being "born again". To give your life to Christ, it requires your willingness to submit yourself to Christ. This process of answering an altar call requires that somebody will make a call for people that want to give their life to Christ.

When a person answers such a call by coming out openly to identify himself with the people of God, the person has taken the first step. In most cases, Christians believe that the moment someone answers an altar call, the fellow has become born again. Born again is not an automatic thing. In some cases, the person makes the fellow that answers the altar call often says some short prayer like: 'Lord Jesus, come into my life, wash me with your blood for I am a sinner. Today, I receive you as my Lord and personal saviour'.

The Pastor may declare: 'Now, you are born again' or "'thank God, you are born again".

Please, that does not make such a fellow born again. Rather, the fellow has taken the first step towards "being christian".

GOING THROUGH BELIEVERS' CLASS (BAPTISMAL CLASS/TRAINING)

After confessing Jesus openly or answering an altar call, the next step is to join the believers or baptismal class where the fellow is taught everything he needs to know in order to grow.

'Like a new born babe, desire the sincere milk' (1 Peter 2v2).

If you look at this statement, you will understand that a new born baby cannot be born again. Why? This is because the baby never know what life is all about. So, the decision of being born again cannot be possible for such a baby.

It is in the believer's class that the person will be taught the fundamentals of Christianity and how Satan operates to deceive believers. It is through this process of training that the fellow gets matured in Christian life and decides totally either to continue or to quit.

BAPTISM

After the baptismal class, the next is Baptism proper. Baptism proper is a period where the fellow is prepared to be used by God. It makes a person part of Christ or part of God's family.

Even our Lord Jesus did not jump that process. When he went to John the Baptist, John confirmed that he should not have come to him for baptism, but Jesus told him that it must be done to fulfill all righteousness. In other word, no one jumps a stage or a process if really the fellow wants to be "born again".

Some lay hands on such a fellow before being baptized; some baptize before laying hands on the fellow. The most important thing to note is that laying of hands is the period where fire is transferred from the vessel laying the hand to the fellow being prepared for use. It can come before baptism or after baptism by immersion.

Now, through the laying of hands and baptism, the fellow has caught the fire. Also, remember that during the process of baptism, the person is buried in the water signifying his death and burial of our Lord Jesus; the person is raised, signifying the resurrection of Jesus.

CONTINUOUS FELLOWSHIPPING WITH BELIEVERS (CONSTANT STUDY OF THE WORD, LISTENING TO MESSAGES FROM TRUSTED SOURCES).

After the baptism and laying of hands, the fellow will constantly study the word, fellowship with others in order to grow.

Remember, before Holy Ghost descended, Christ told his disciples to stay in a place before he ascended into heaven. They were there exalting one another in the word, learning, listening to one another until they caught the fire and became transformed.

It is always the period of fellowship, study of the word and exercising the authority in the word that makes one born like fire.

In other words, that makes you born again. You are not born again by declaration. You are not born again by telling people that you are born again. You are born again by burning like fire, so, that the enemies will run away from you.

SPIRITUAL GROWTH

When you begin to fellowship and study the word, you will experience fire burning all over you. You will no more be like a new born baby, you are now mature.

This process varies from one person to another. Some people experience rapid spiritual development, but some do not.

Spiritual growth depends on the individual. You can develop spiritual gift rapidly; this depends on you. Some people gave their life to Christ ten years earlier yet, they are still lost in the congregation. Some gave their lives, six months after, they are mature and even qualified to be ordained.

When you receive the fire during the laying of hands, after baptism and constant fellowship with believers, you need to speed up your spiritual growth.

The most advisable pattern to spiritual growth is evangelism. Preach to people. It is a sign that you have caught the fire.

No wonder the bible says: **'He that winneth a soul is wise'.** As you develop the habit of talking to people about Christ, you will discover a very rapid spiritual growth.

BURNING LIKE FIRE

When you have developed spiritually, you become fire. You manifest the gift of the Spirit. That is the period called **"born again"**. You don't need to tell your enemies that you are now fire and not dust.

At this stage, the bible says that believers are endowed with the spirit of boldness and a sound mind **(2 Timothy 1v7)**. At this point, Satan runs away when he hears that you are coming. You become a terror to Satan and agents of darkness.

CHAPTER SIX

How To Become Fire

To become fire, you must understand what fire is. You must know what fire is all about and you must know the purpose of becoming fire.

Fire is a force that burns down the camp of the enemies without leaving any object standing. The enemy knows that fire is meant for their destruction; even Satan knows that by the end, he will be thrown into fire, he makes every effort to take as many sinners as possible with him.

Fire is a direct enemy to Satan. The presence of fire makes Satan uncomfortable. Fire is a force in you that fights against your enemy.

It may not be that kind of fire you use in cooking. It may not be that kind you use to light up your candle, it is a force that makes a believer to resist the presence of the enemy. It makes a believer not to compromise with the enemy.

There are numerous instances believers were held at gun point because of the gospel and asked to deny Christ but such threat never moved them. It is not as a result of the fellow being strong but as a result of fire in that fellow.

Fire is all about the ignition that energizes a believer to do that which he/she could not do ordinarily. **Acts of the Apostles 2v14.**

From verse 1, you will see how fire came upon the

apostles and disciples and in verse 14, you will see how it gave Peter the energy and boldness to speak.

The Bible says in verse 41 that 3,000 people gave their life to Christ as a result of Peter's boldness in declaring the word.

Fire can be likened as a **'FORCEFUL IGNITION REBUILDING ENERGY'**. The primary function of fire in the life of a believer is to boost your energy.

When you are praying, if there is a presence of fire, you will discover that within six hours, it will look like six minutes. Why? It is because of the presence of fire.

If there is no fire, just pray for five minutes and you will become tired. Fire also makes a believer bold. When there is fire, you can stand in front of any force without fear. For example, those believers that always fight against the devil are fearless and strong.

Imagine you are praying a dangerous prayer; suddenly, a dragon appears. How many of the so called believers can stand? It is not going to be easy without the presence of fire. When there is fire, you can withstand any force.

No matter how many hours you can pray, no matter how many days you can fast, without fire, it is just in vain. No wonder some people go for deliverance twice or more, but the demon afflicting still persist in the life of such fellows.

If there is no fire in such fellows, they are mere meat to the demon. Whoever says because the meat in your pot is half-cooked so, it is no more his food?

One may go through deliverance time without number, but as long as he has not caught the fire, he is still dust. Even if all the men of God on earth hold prayer for such a fellow, as long as he has not caught the fire, he still remains dust.

The first step to execute deliverance is to give one's life to Christ. Once Christ takes over one's life, no demon can live in that life. The issue is that giving one's life to Christ is not as easy as we think. Before one gives one's life to Christ, one must ask for God's grace.

Jesus made it open that some people are not of His sheep fold. Even in **Matthew 7v21,** He said that not all that calls Him Lord, Lord will enter into the Kingdom of God.

Giving one's life to Christ is a total surrendering all to Him. In other words, all one does on earth is to lift His name. When one gives one's life to Him, one always announces Him in all one does.

Constant fellowship and study of the word ignite the fire in you and naturally drive out all manner of evil forces in you.

When you become fire, the Holy Spirit makes you a partner. He is fire, God is fire, so nothing stops you; even water cannot stop you.

This kind of fire cannot be quenched by water because this fire has power to walk upon water, **(Matthew 14v25;** Jesus walked upon water). This means that water becomes fuel to the fire.

When you become fire, fire cannot burn you, because you have become a son to fire. Example, Shedrach, Meshach and Abadnego **(Daniel 3v11-25).** One significant thing about these boys was that they were thrown into the fire and the fire refused to burn them.

The secret there is that they are the children of fire.

'For God is a consuming fire' (Hebrew 12v29).

Now tell me, how can their father consume them?

If you read closely that bible verse, you will discover that they made one fire and throw in three fires and the total fire became four.

> **'Then Nebuchadnezzar the king was astonished, and rose up in haste, and spake, and said unto his counsellors, Did not we cast three men bound into the midst of the fire? They answered and said**

unto the king, True, O king. He answered and said, Lo, I see four men loose, walking in the midst of the fire, and they have no hurt; and the form of the fourth is like the Son of God. (Daniel 3v24-25)

So, the intensity of the fire became four times stronger and the heat devoured the men that threw them in.

In the case of Daniel, you discovered that because his father is a lion and a son of a lion is a lion, when he was thrown into the den of lions, the lions in the den saw him as another lion.

They welcomed him as their brother. If you look at it very well, you will discover that they were asking him what he brought for them, because they were very hungry and Daniel said to them; 'Don't worry, I am going out tomorrow and I will bring you plenty of meat'.

When he made that statement, they started rubbing their bodies round Daniel until the following day, when Daniel was taken out.

As the families of the enemies of Daniel were thrown into the den, the bible said that, the lions did not wait for them to fall on the ground before they tore them to pieces because they believed that they were the meat Daniel promised to give to them if he came out of the den. **(Daniel 6v7-24)**

In the case of the apostles, the bible recorded that fire came upon them and instead of consuming them, they were given extra energy to lift the Kingdom of God to the whole world. No wonder Master Jesus asked them to wait until the fire comes.

In the case of Paul, the fire came upon him when he was going to Damascus to destroy the believers and immediately he was converted from Saul to Paul. Fire made him one of the strongest and most active Apostle of Christ.

To become a fire, there are different ways for different

people. Let us consider some of the ways that somebody can receive fire after giving his life to Christ, and is baptized:

1. Direct from the Father
2. Direct transfer through laying of hands
3. From a mentor as a protégée
4. Through evangelism
5. Through study

CHAPTER SEVEN

DUST YOU ARE, DUST YOU SHALL RETURN

There is a statement common among Christians during burial ceremony; **'Dust you are, dust you shall return'.**

If you are born again, you are not dust and you cannot return to dust. When a born again child of God is buried, the person returns to heaven which is his home because the person is a fire; as smoke returns to sky, so a born again Christian returns to heaven.

Return is a personal movement but burial is about other people moving a dead body into the grave.

It is after a person is buried that the decision of where the person goes comes up. If you are fire, you return to heaven, if you are dust, you return to hell as food for Satan. No wonder why the bible said after death comes judgment **(Hebrew 9v27).**

In the book of Hebrew1v7;

'And of the angels he saith, Who maketh his angels spirits, and his ministers a flame of fire'

God made his children flaming fire. That is burning fire; fire that can consume anything including water.

Are you a fire? Fire is the most essential ingredient that is really dying down in our Christian life today.

'And Enoch lived sixty and five years, and begat Methuselah. And Enoch walked with God after he begat Methuselah. And Enoch walked with God after he begat Methuselah three hundred years, and begat sons and daughters. And all the days of Enoch were three hundred and sixty and five years. And Enoch walked with God and he was not for God took him'. (Genesis 5v21-24).

Constant fellowship with God turned Enoch to fire, that is, total commitment to God turns a man to a flaming fire.

When we hear such stories, at times, we wonder if they are true. Did it really happen? Our doubt can be cleared when we begin to study the life of the Christian martyrs.

Imagine how a group of the martyrs were kept at a place like a stadium and lions were let loose on them and they did not denounce Christ until the lions devoured all of them.

They cannot withstand those period by flesh. It is only by constant fellowship with God which leads to transformation from dust to fire that can give them the courage to withstand such situations.

The bible said that Enoch did not die. How can he see death? Imagine somebody that was walking with God everyday for more than three hundred years.

If he was a pot in a potter's fire for such a period and did not burst, he would have been turned to an unbreakable pot.

That is total transformation from dust to fire and from fire to pure fire.

Iron sharpens iron. And one man sharpens another. Proverb 27v17

If this statement is true, we can easily understand why

God took Enoch. Fire can sharpen fire. Enoch became fire due to his constant fellowship with God for more than three hundred years. God might have sharpened him to the level that he was transformed to the heavenly beings and he could no longer live on earth.

Elijah responded to the captain of the fifty men that came to arrest him; "If I be a man of God, let fire come down from heaven and consume you and your fifty men" 2kings 1v10

The fire came down from heaven and consumed him and his fifty men.

If you are not fire, you cannot call down fire, it takes fire to call down fire, because fire begets fire.

As a Christian, shout fire from now till the next one year, fire will not answer you unless you are fire. God is fire, so His children ought to be fire. If you are dust you are not a child of God; you are just a meal for Satan.

Elijah was able to call down fire because he is fire. Elijah did not see death, because he is fire. He returned to heaven without death just like that because he was transformed from dust to fire and from fire to pure fire.

When our Lord Jesus Christ was crucified, he was buried. After the burial, He resurrected. After the resurrection, He ascended to heaven as King of kings.

Jesus Christ is fire. He transformed all his Disciples to fire. He knows that no man can overcome the pleasure of this world without being fire; that was why he told his Disciples to stay at a place until the fire came to lit them up.

The moment they caught the fire, they were able to boldly face tribulations. Fire is not only necessary to our Christian faith but compulsory.

No man can serve God in truth and in spirit through flesh and blood. To serve God in truth and in spirit you must become fire and you must keep burning until the end of days.

Fire is what makes you a Christian, that is, Christianity minus fire is equal to carnality. When a Christian becomes fire, the enemies become afraid of the fellow including his properties and whatsoever is dear to him.

CHAPTER EIGHT

You Want Prosperity?

The bible says that it is God that gives us power to make wealth **(Deuteronomy 8v18).** Power to make wealth is not from numerous prosperity teachings around the world today.

People are thrilled when they listen to prosperity teachings. I discovered that out of ten prosperity books and seminars, only few people benefit, from reading them or attending such seminars.

Those teachings are human calculations and philosophy. They may work, or they may not work.

Real prosperity comes from God. It is unconditional and can come in any form because God does not work with the traditions of men. It is only men that have specific patterns of doing things.

The moment you meet the standard of God, He releases His blessing upon you.

Then, if you are able to become fire, you will be given the power to make wealth and your wealth will be protected by fire because you are fire.

The reason why most people cannot prosper in life is because their glory has been taken away by the forces of darkness legally; but they are not aware of the problem.

Sometimes, the glory of a person might not have been taken away but the kingdom of darkness has formed a road block against such a person. It becomes difficult for such a person to pass through the road to greatness.

Imagine someone trying to go somewhere, and the police force, or army, or even criminals blocked the road that leads to his/her destination.

What do you expect that person to do? It is either the person turns back or the forces hijack the persons, collect the person's entire belongings and even, kill such a person.

It is a very serious matter. At times, one may attend seminars or leadership training, or workshop on how to become rich, read books about prosperity, apply all the principles one is taught, yet nothing happens. One is advised to go for deliverance.

Deliverance does not mean drawing someone out of trouble alone, it means showing a person a way to pass towards fulfilling a destiny. In so many cases, when someone undergoes deliverance, the person sits at home doing nothing.

The bible said that when an unclean spirit is cast out of a person, it will go, turn back to see if the place is still vacant for him. If it is empty, he will go gather stronger demons than him to occupy the place **(Luke 11v26).**

There are things that should be put into consideration when conducting deliverance.

Deliverance is another stronger person showing a lesser person the way to prosperity in Christ through prayers principles.

It is when the stronger person makes it clear to the lesser person that prayer has levels and that in prayer, there is difference between request and order.

In prayer we have;
1. Praise and Worship
2. Thanksgiving
3. Confession
4. Supplication
5. Warfare. **(Exodus 15v3);** The Lord is a man of war

Deliverance means taking someone away from the forces of darkness into the marvelous light of Christ. It is a period of transformation from darkness to light, from dust to fire.

Many so-called deliverance ministers make such mistake. After delivering a person from the dark powers into light, they never bothered about the continuous spiritual life of such a fellow.

If the person delivered never turned from dust to fire, there is the possibility that the enemy will always come back to take the person captive again. Until a man is converted from dust to fire, he is still a meal for the devil.

Even if you occupy any position in the church, you are still a dust, you remain unprotected by God. The moment you become fire, all things the enemy have collected will be forcefully restored to you, even in multiple folds.

I have seen instances where the enemy contested with the deliverance minister. The enemy usually questions the authority of the deliverance minister,

"Jesus I know, Paul I know, who are you"? (Act 19v15)

It is a vital question. Very often, Satan knows you better than you know yourself. Satan knows the children of God and the pretenders. If you are born again, they know; if you are dust, they know; if you are fire, they know.

Jesus I know, Paul I know, who are you? Jesus is a fire, Paul is a fire, but who are you? Are you fire or a dust? It simply means that before you conduct deliverance on someone, you must be sure of who you are.

If you are not sure, please stay away. A woman went to conduct deliverance of a small girl. As she laid her hand on the girl, she became insane.

Can a fowl or a cow or an elephant context with the owner when they know that they are just ordinary meat to the owner?

The owner has the right to kill the meat for meal or to sell the meat for money and nobody queries him; so is a man that is still a dust to the devil. If you are not sure of yourself, please never ever try to lay hands on a person possessed of evil spirit.

In the book of **Deuteronomy 6v24;**

> **"The Lord commands us to follow all these statutes and to fear the Lord our God for our prosperity always and for our preservation as it is today"**

If you read through Deuteronomy 6, from chapter one, you will discover that Moses spoke about the statutes and ordinances of the Lord very much. Whenever he talks about those commandments, he lays emphasis on obedience and not work or sacrifice.

In this verse 24, he made it clear that the Lord God commands us to follow all the ordinances and fear him so that we may prosper always and not only prosper, but that he will protect us.

If you read **Deuteronomy chapter 28** you will discover that verse 1-13, is full of blessings but from verse 14 to the end is about curses on people that do not obey God.

In the book of **1Samuel 2v7-8;**

> **"The Lord brings prosperity and gives wealth; He humbles and He exalts; He raises the poor from the dust and lifts the needy from the garbage pile. He seats them with nobles and gives them a throne of honour, for the foundation of the earth are the Lord's; He has set the world on them"**

As a matter of fact, it is not all these human philosophies about wealth that really make a man wealthy. It is possible that you enjoy those philosophies and even apply all the principles on them and still, remain poor.

1Samuel 2 v7-8 tells us that poverty and wealth come from the Lord.

You have to obey God to have prosperity. During the Old Testament life, it looks as if obeying God was difficult, but in this new testament, all you need is Jesus in your life. He will convert you from dust to fire, and all you are seeking for will come to you.

In the book of

Matthew 6v33;

"But seek first the kingdom of God and His righteousness, and all these things will be added to you"

Seek the kingdom of God first, every other thing will be added to you. But the issue is what is the kingdom of God that we should seek and how can we seek this kingdom?

Kingdom is a word that is made up of two words, king and dom; that is king and domain. King as we know is a great controller, ruler, and leader. Domain means a specified territory.

So, combined king and domain together, you will get a territory that God controls, rules and leads. Kingdom means Gods own territory.

In the book of;

1Corinthians 4v20;

"For the kingdom of God is not in talk but in demonstration of power"

The Kingdom of God has to do with a territory where God can demonstrate His supremacy, authority and power.

So, when we hear **"seek you first his kingdom",** we must understand that the bible is talking about us making ourselves available to God to demonstrate His power, authority and supremacy.

That is why the bible said that our body is the temple of the Holy Spirit, **(1 Corinthians 6v19).** So, when you make your body the temple of the Holy Spirit, it simply means that you have found the kingdom of God.

Your life will automatically become a place where God demonstrates His power, authority and supremacy. Then, if you talk about wealth, this will overflow, followed by protection, divine favour and power over the enemies of life.

How do you seek His kingdom? By accepting Jesus as your personal Lord and savior, you have made yourself a part of Christ body.

The moment a person received Christ and followed the steps of being born again, the person is automatically converted from dust to fire.

God cannot dwell in the dust because He is fire, dust cannot carry God. So, if you are a dust, you are not of God and you have not found His kingdom.

If you are fire, God dwells in you, because likes-begets-likes. Before your body will be the temple of the Holy Spirit, it means that you have been converted from dust which can never be the temple of the Holy Spirit, to fire which can carry God's presence.

You will discover that the moment a man became fire or found the kingdom of God, everything about him will change for better.

You are no more operating from the physical realm that has much limitation, rather from the spiritual realm which has no limitation.

That is a period when whatever man seeks, he gets because God is in him and the power, authority and supremacy of God dwell with the fellow.

You do not force people to respect you, you do not force demons to obey you, you do not force blessing to come to you, all you need is to get God into your life and all these things have no choice but to obey you without hestitation.

CHAPTER NINE

SATANIC ACTIVITIES AGAINST CHRISTIANITY

You have heard some kinds of mysterious deaths of people now and then. Consider these few ones;

A bus moving down the road, missed its lane and fell into the sea with all the passengers on board; no one came out alive.

A woman and her husband watched their four children burnt to death. Four children from the same parents drowned in the river as they went home for a Christmas celebration.

Have you considered the cases of terrorists around the world? How some of them burnt down churches and killed innocent people with the intention of doing the will of their god.

Have you considered all kinds of accidents including plane crashes, boat capsizing and such a likes around the world?

Many people die per day. Some just had slight headache, the next is death. Others have sicknesses of all kinds. Whether you know it or not, whether you believe it or not, the way you go to your pen, take a goat, slaughter it and make pepper soup; the way you go to your ranch, take a cow, butcher it for food; the way you go to a poultry pick up a fowl, kill and eat it, so you are to Satan, if you are still a dust.

The only remedy is to be born again. "Born again" is the period when a soul is converted from dust to fire. That is, from food to Satan, to his direct enemy which is fire.

There is nothing that makes the devil afraid than fire. He knows that at the end, he will be thrown into hell fire. It is because of the fear of hell fire that he drags as many as he could to join him.

When we hear this kind of news, some may be tempted to doubt the existence of God or even ask God, where He was when these things were happening? I want to bring the answer to whoever cares to know.

The answer is that God is a God of order, and principle. He cannot give you something and take that thing away from you again. That is why the bible said that the gift of God has no repentance **(Roman 11v29).**

God has already given man to Satan as food. So, whenever Satan takes away a man and eat, God cannot be held responsible.

If a man goes into his poultry farm and takes a fowl, kills and eats, has he committed any sin? Of course not. So, as far as God is concerned, man is dust and dust is food for Satan.

No wonder, God sent Jesus Christ to die for us to redeem man back from being dust, the food to Satan but to fire, the direct enemy to Satan.

The bible said;

"For God so love the world that He gave His only begotten Son that whosoever believeth in Him will not die but have everlasting life" John 3v16.

It is only dust that dies, fire cannot die, and so if a man

accepts Jesus as his personal Lord and Saviour, the person has been converted from dust to fire.

If you listen to some testimonies, you will hear how people were saved from disasters. How people escaped from the trap of ritual killers and things like that.

Some people were caught in the trap of ritual killers; some of them were released, while some were killed. Those that were release gave their testimonies and from their testimonies, the ritual killers quarrel among themselves over why they brought those kinds of people to their den.

Those kinds of testimonies can only come to those that are born again. Those that have been transformed from dust to fire because Satan can only eat dust and no matter how he tries, he cannot eat fire because fire will burn him.

We hear of earthquakes, hurricanes of different kinds, flood and so many other natural disasters, even wars and political unrest all over the world. People fear when they hear such news.

Some have doubt about the existence of God, whether we know it or not, whether we believe it or not, God is real. He has set His world in order, if you like, follow Him and be saved.

He said;

> **'I call heaven and earth to record this day against you, that I have set before you life and death, blessing and cursing: therefore choose life, that both thou and thy seed may live'(Deuteronomy 30:19).**

The greatest thing God did for humanity is Christ Jesus. We may know it, we may not know it. Many Continents would have been wasted if not for Christ. Roasting and eating human being would not have stopped legally in some parts of the world today.

I read the account of Moses in the book of Deuteronomy;

I ask myself why God commanded the people of Israel to kill everybody, not to remain one single soul in every nation He gave them for possession.

Does it mean that God love seeing people die? I discovered that all those nations worship idols, and kill their children for ritual. They do so many abominable things against God and are always challenge the authority of the supreme God, because of their gods.

God hates idol worshipping so much that He can wipe off entire generations because of it. He hates it, the world belongs to Him and He cannot share His Glory with satan and any kind of man-made gods.

When a man worships idol, the man has given his life to Satan willingly and Satan has no pity on people because he feeds on them.

Little does man know that he is a food, legally provided to Satan. So he always does things that puts him into the cage of the devil.

Many philosophers even argue that there is no God anywhere. They claim that we were being deceived by the teaching of resurrection of the dead. To them, man is dust, so, man is born, and he lives for some years and dies, and returns to dust.

I want to bring good news to you today, God did not create man as dust. **It was as a result of Adam's sin that He turned man to dust.**

The first Adam sinned against God and God turned him to dust. **Turning man to dust is the Adamic sin we often hear.** Many believe that because through sexual intercourse man is born, sex makes man commit Adamic sin.

No Adamic sin is the curse God placed on man of being a dust as Adam is a dust. As long as you are born of a woman, you are a dust and that is the Adamic sin. When you are a dust, you remain food for Satan.

The last Adam **(Christ)** came. He also came through a woman. He became a dust. He knew it. That was why John the Baptist was sent before Him to make way for Him. The bible said that John began to baptize everybody with just water warning them to repent and come to God.

When Christ came to him for baptism, he never wanted to baptize him, rather, John wanted Christ to baptize him, but Jesus understands all things so he insisted on the baptism. After the baptism, heaven opened and God spoke;

"This is my beloved son in Him I am well pleased, listen to Him" (Matthew 3v17).

This did not end there, the bible recorded that after the baptism, the spirit of God took Him direct to the wilderness. He stayed there transformed himself to fire by praying and fasting and in communion with God, the Father because He knew that the Baptism of John was not enough to withstand the claim of Satan over man.

After fasting for forty days and forty nights, Satan came to test Him. All gold are tried in fire. Actually, Satan wanted to find out if He was still a dust. The moment Satan discovered that this man was no more a dust, he has become fire, Satan sensed danger.

Since then, Christ can walk up to a Satan-possessed person and cast out the devil because he is fire. When a demon possessed man saw him coming, the demon in the man would begin to plead because they saw the fire in Him.

So, the first Adam became dust by sin of disobedience, the last Adam became fire by work of obedience.

The second Adam made it open that whosoever believeth in Him will not die. It simply means that if you believe in Christ Jesus, as your Personal Lord and savior and you are ready to obey him totally, He will transform you from dust to fire and that is what is called born again.

Except a man is born again, he cannot enter the kingdom of God. Dust cannot enter God's kingdom no matter how you try because even if you enter as a dust, you will pollute the environment and of course we know God hates dirt.

Some religious sects are determined to wipe off the entire Christian race. They hate Christianity to such an extent that they are ready to kill everybody called a Christian.

They were supported by their own god and claim it is in their own book to wipe off any nation that will not bow down to their god, and they are working very hard to accomplish that goal.

Sadly enough, many Christian nations are relaxing so much that fire has gone out of them totally. In Christian churches today, sexual immoralities have been legalized with sweet name; 'gay **(man marries man and woman marries woman),** the church even weds them and gives them certificate of marriage. That is a satanic lie. It has gone to the extent of man wedding a dog.

The intention is to provoke God to leave his own children alone so that the religious sect that vowed to destroy Christianity will succeed.

These people are doing all they could to destroy United States of America the way they destroyed Soviet Union. If they succeed, it will be very terrible for Christian nations all over the world.

Christianity is getting colder everyday, no more revival fire in the church. Denomination fighting denomination, politics in the church of Christ are tearing churches apart. But Jesus said that gate of hell will not prevail against the church of God. **Matt. 16v18**

Some Church people are forming alliances with their enemy to destroy the work of Christ, God forbid. Fire must return to the church if Christians want to really win the battle.

The fire is not made for general overseers alone, but for everyone that is called of God as a Christian.

CHAPTER TEN

Jesus Is Coming Soon

So many believers are afraid when they hear that statement; **"Jesus is coming soon"**. Some do not even want him to come again.

Some are very happy when they hear that their Lord is coming soon. Some are seeing the statement as what cannot happen because of the long waiting since **0033AD**. Till date, we still hear, Jesus is coming soon.

Are we sure that he has not come and gone? Are we sure they are not deceiving us? Then, what is delaying his coming if it is true?

You see, there are two categories of wives in this setting, because the bible calls the church the bride of Christ.

One is the adulterous and way-ward wife. She saw her husband travelled to a far country; she saw it as an opportunity to carry out her enterprise. She went out with different men; drank all manner of alcoholic drinks; smoke; went to night parties and enjoyed herself.

When she heard that her husband was coming back, she is not excited; she frowned: "Oh why so soon, he would have waited for some more time, he would have even not come back again. If he comes now, he would not allow me to live my normal life. Our neighbours will tell him all I have been doing.

Anyway, as far as I am concerned, I must continue with my normal life. If he likes, let him divorce me all I care. If he likes let him even die so that I will have my liberty" **(Songs of Solomon 7).**

This woman is never excited to hear that her husband is coming back.

The second category of wives is a virtuous woman, woman of honour and integrity, woman that values God more than rupees, gold or jewelries. She sees her home first and makes it better than others.

She does not listen to gossips; she is always found in the house of God; she hates immorality. When her husband travels, she starts missing him immediately.

When she hears that he is coming back soon, she makes the bed, cooks the most favorite meal, cleans the house, and herself and even goes ahead to invite her sisters and brothers, her mother and father, her friends and relatives that her husband is coming back soon.

If the man tells her that he is coming back the next one week, she sees the one week as seven years. It becomes too far for her; she will be restless until the weekend. If after the one week, she did not see her lover, she makes phone calls, gets worried, and opens her ears to get information about any problems on the way. She will be sleepless until she hears her lover's voice. **(Book of Proverbs 31).**

If you are a truly born again child of God, I think one thing you must not be afraid of is his coming. He always talks to his own because the bible calls him the comforter.

He always sends a message of comfort across to his own children. His own do not really get worried about his coming; they get worried about doing those things they know he will love if he is around. They do those things he loves doing when he was not around, they are not eye-service people.

Look at it from this angle; 'The bible said that he is

coming for both the living and the dead. During that period, the dead will rise first **(1 Thessalonians 4v16)**.

If this statement is true, then why are we worried about whether he will come or not. When we live a life that is pleasing to him and dies, let it be thousands of years and he comes, we are still coming out to meet him.

When we live a life unpleasing to him, when we die, let it be thousands of years before he comes, we are still coming out to face him. Then, why not forget about the worry of his coming and make our life pleasing to him.

I think the best way to live such life is to pattern our life after the second category of woman that heard that her husband was coming soon, made every arrangement to welcome him, even invited her family members, relatives and friends.

If we live our life as if he is coming the next moment, we will discover that we will get more prepared to receive him when he eventually comes, whether we are alive or not. This is better than getting unnecessarily worried about his coming.

He said he knows his sheep and his sheep knows him; they hear his voice and he hears their voice, **(John 10v14)**. It simply means that there are people that hear his voice till date.

It also means that he communicates with people about his coming. So, if he is not communicating with you about his coming, it simply means either you are not part of him at all or you are still a dust. How can you hear him when you are not a fire?

When some believers hear the rapture, they become scared. Though it is the way some people paint the scene of rapture to us that makes many believers never wanted to witness the rapture.

The funny thing is that, as long as you are a human being, whether alive or dead, you must face rapture, because the bible said that the dead in Christ shall rise first before the living in Christ rise.

Both the dead and the living in Christ will be caught up in heaven to meet with the Lord coming down for the marriage ceremony.

If it is true, why are we not worried about the way we spend our life here on earth? Instead of being concerned about what we cannot control.

Spend your life as if he is coming to take you in the next minute; spend your life as, even, if he did not come to take you alive, you are still going to join him from the grave when he comes.

The Hebrew boys, said even if their God would not come to rescue them, they would never bow down to the idol **(Daniel 3v16-18).**

To follow Christ, you must take up your cross. It is for better for worse, that is marriage. Marriage is never for better for best, it is for better for worse, so we should follow him.

Whether he is coming, whether rapture is going to take place or not, I have decided to follow Jesus, no going back, no going back, this should be our song always.

If you can make up your mind to this extent, you are already a fire for Christ. You will see yourself burning down all the plans of the enemies around you.

So many people are worried about the end of the world. Some say they have been hearing about the end of the world for many years but the world has not ended. Why are you worried about the end of the world? What is your business about that? What if the creator of the world decides that he does not want to end the world again, what will you do? So, will you call him a liar?

Jesus said to James and John when they came to plead for Christ to allow them sit at his right and left side in heaven because they saw that Christ loved John specially and being that James and John were twin brothers, they made that request; Christ told them that it is not his decision to select who sits where in heaven; it is totally his Father's decision. **(Mark 10v35-40)**

Following Christ has so many benefits apart from making heaven. There are many reasons you must follow him. These reasons can be classified under the three Ps that makes man seek God; they are Power, Protection and Provision.

So, apart from making heaven which is the number one reason for following him, he will also give you power to make wealth **(Deut 8V18)**, he will give you power to defeat your internal and external enemies.

When you follow him, he will protect you from both internal and external enemies, both seen and unseen enemies **(Psalm 91 and Psalm 23)**.

If you trample upon serpent and scorpion, they will not hurt you. Nothing shall by any means hurt you (Luke 10v19).

If you follow him, you will not lack because he is your provider **(Deuteronomy 30:19)**.

If all these things are true, then why worry about whether the world will end or not? Some people go on committing sin because they see the story of the end of the world as hearsay.

To make the whole matter worse, some people claim that they know the date the world will end. When these dates passed and nothing happened, it made the doubting souls get more reasons not to believe in Christ.

Whether they believe it or not, whether they know it or not, the world will end one day. It is either a man dies and his world ends or God takes his decision and closes-up the folder called world.

So, whichever way, we should not get worried about what we cannot control. We should get worried about how we spend our life, either as a fire or dust.

Christ is so gracious that he cares about your life here on earth. He wants you to finish well on earth. He is interested in your success here on earth. He said;

'I wish above all that you may prosper and be of good health' (3 John 1v2).

What a loving Lord? Can you ever find such love on earth? Ask people worshipping other gods, they kill their worshippers mercilessly. Yes of course, if you are an idol worshipper or a Satanist, you are a dust, just a meal to the devil. Satan does not value your life.

He kills at any time without pity. At slightest provocation, you are gone. In fact, the major difference between the kingdom of God and the kingdom of darkness is love.

There is no love in the kingdom of darkness. They hate one another, that is why at times, they fight themselves. So, they don't care if you are dying or not.

It is not their fault, their followers are like chicken to them. They feed on those that follow them and those that do not belong to Christ.

Christ is full of love; not only that, he has compassion for the sinners and the sick, the down trodden and the demon possessed. He gave his life for all.

It would have been his wish if everybody accepts his offer to be saved but because Satan is still contesting over man that is why Christ made it open that whoever accepts him will not die or perish. **(John 3v16), (John 6v40).**

If you accept him, he will make you a fire. He will convert you from being a meal to Satan to becoming a terror to Satan, from dust to fire. Accept him today and have a life full of success, full of joy, full of good health, full of peace and full of hope for eternity.

CHAPTER ELEVEN

What Makes The Difference

Every religion on earth is directed towards God. Some believe that going to God through Christ is a man-made doctrine. Some argue that God is our Father, and then we should go to Him direct. Christians believe that the word of our Lord Jesus Christ is the truth when he said that;

"no man cometh to the Father except through me" (John 14v6).

The question is, what did he mean when he made that statement?'No man cometh to the Father except through me'. If you read through the Old Testament, before Christ era, people have been going to God and God has been coming to man **(Judges 16v11-16).**

Then, why suddenly one man came out from nowhere and began to claim that no man cometh to the Father except through him? Does it mean that people have not been going to God or God has not been coming to man?

As a matter of fact, the statement seems questionable. In fact, Christ did not just make that statement, he started to tell us that he is the way, the truth and the life.

So, to him, he is the way to God, the way to true prosperity, the way to righteous life, the way to holiness, the way to heaven, the way to spiritual freedom, and the way to physical freedom.

Then what is a way? A way can be defined as a path or direction leading to a place. If you are going to a place you have never been, you will pay attention to the sign post for direction.

The arrows and direction on the sign post leads you through to the place you are going without asking anybody for direction. If there is no sign post, you will ask people around for direction.

When the people of Israel were going to the Promised Land, the bible said that God was with them in the form of a pillar of cloud by the day time and in the form of a pillar of fire in the night time to direct them through the journey because they did not know the way to their destination.

Christ is the pillar of cloud and the pillar of fire that was directing the people of Israel. He is the sign post you need to excel in life, he is the arrow pointer that you need to fulfill destiny in this life, and he is the right person to ask for direction that will not mislead you.

He is the way, if you follow Christ, Satan will not make a meal of you, you will live a fulfilled life on earth and have eternal life in heaven with your Maker.

He is the way and his teachings and way of life is directed towards saving you from the power of darkness to the marvelous light of our God. Then why not follow him now. Become born again and be converted from dust to fire.

He is the truth. The big question here is, what is the meaning of 'Truth'? If we can get the meaning of the word "Truth", then it will become easier for us to understand what he meant by saying that he is the truth.

The 'Truth' is a statement, declaration or an action directed towards saving a man or a situation. That is, when you say something is the truth, it means that the thing is directed towards saving a situation or a life.

On the other hand, when you say something is a lie,

it means that such a thing is directed towards destroying a situation or a life. When somebody tells the truth with the intension of destroying another innocent person, that person becomes a liar.

Often times, when Satan comes to deceive a man, he tells the man the truth but with the intention of destroying the man. Satan knows that one of our weapons of warfare is the truth **(Ephesians 6v12-17),** so, if he wants to catch a man, he begins by telling the truth.

Example. When Satan visited Eve, his first statement was the truth; **'Did God say you should not eat of these fruit'?** Eve answered; 'Yes, he said so'. Then, Eve explained the reason God said so. Satan then said; **"No, you will not die, but you will be like God".** If you read **Genesis 2v15-17** when God told Adam not to eat the fruit, God made it clear that when he eats the fruit, he will die and he will have the knowledge of good and evil.

Satan told her that she would not die but her eyes would be open to know the difference between the good and the evil and that she will be like God **(Genesis 3v4).** Look at it, from the beginning, God has already told them that they are like Him. Why is Satan telling them that if they eat the fruit they will be like God.

It was the same trick he (Satan) wanted to use for Christ during the temptation in **Matthew 4v2.** He said to Christ;

'If you are a son of God command this stone to become bread'

Of course, he (Satan) knew that Christ just finished fasting so, he (Christ) might have been hungry. This is an issue of identity. Knowing who you are.

Christ knew from beginning that he (Christ) is the son of God, so, he (Christ) needed nobody to tell him that he (Christ) is the son of God.

The bible said that the weapon of our warfare is not carnal but spiritual and one of the weapon is truth.

All spiritual media tell the truth about a situation or to a person that visits them. The religion that believes that man can go to God direct tells the truth, but the basis of their truth are directed toward destruction.

It is because most spirits that come to hunt men for food come by telling the man the truth about him or herself. This makes the man to believe the spirit and finds himself inside the pot of pepper soup of that spirit. That is the reason why the bible, through the gift of the Holy Spirit, tells us to test all spirits before believing any story from them, **(1John 4v1)**.

This makes the gift of discerning of spirits so important as far as Christianity is concerned. Jesus said, he is the truth. Yes, he is the truth. Why am I very sure?

A man told me that the daughter of the founder of a particular religion on earth went to her father who was lying down on his sick bed waiting for the time to die. The girl asked the father; 'if you die now where are you going? To heaven or to hell'. The man answered; 'My daughter, I don't know where I am going, it is only God that decides that'.

Our dearly Beloved Jesus Christ, when his time came he told his disciples that he was going to his Father;

'I am going to my father, I am going to prepare a place for you. In my Father's house there many mansions there (John 14v2).

This means that he is very, very, very sure of who he is, where he came from and where he was going.

He is the truth, he said;

> **"The spirit of the Lord is upon me to set the captive free" (Luke 4v18).**

And really, not just that he said so, he did that for the man at the pool of Bethesda **(John 5v5-9);** the man with legion of spirits **(Mark 5v1-16),** Mary Magdalene **(John 8v1-12),** blind Barthemeous **(Mark 10v46-52),** and so many others. He is still in the business of setting the captives free.

The bible said;

> **'If the son shall set you free, you are free indeed (John 8v36).**

He is the truth because he gives you spiritual freedom, that is, if you are in Christ Jesus, you have every right to call God your Father at any time. He also gives physical freedom. All that the enemies stole from you, he must restore, because Satan cannot hold what belongs to Christ.

He heals the sick, even raises the dead. He gives true prosperity that is void of human philosophy. His wealth adds no sorrow. He maketh rich and adds no sorrow **(Proverb 10v22).**

He always exposes the intensions of the enemies, and also reveals the future to his own, that is why he is the truth.

He is the life. This one, among the three, looks as the most controversial statement. Christ told the people of Israel;

> **"He who eats my flesh and drinks my blood will not die; "I am that bread of life. Your fathers did eat manna in the wilderness, and are dead. This is the bread which cometh down from heaven, that a man may eat thereof, and not die. I am the living**

bread which came down from heaven: if any man eat of this bread, he shall live forever: and the bread that I will give is my flesh, which I will give for the life of the world". The Jews therefore strove among themselves, saying, how can this man give us his flesh to eat? Then Jesus said unto them, "Verily, verily, I say unto you, except ye eat the flesh of the Son of man, and drink his blood, ye have no life in you. Whoso eateth my flesh, and drinketh my blood, hath eternal life; and I will raise him up at the last day. For my flesh is meat indeed, and my blood is drink indeed.

He that eateth my flesh, and drinketh my blood, dwelleth in me, and I in him. As the living Father hath sent me, and I live by the Father: so he that eateth me, even he shall live by me. This is that bread which came down from heaven: not as your fathers did eat manna, and are dead: he that eateth of this bread shall live forever" (John 48v58).

The Jewish people nearly killed him that day, even the statement was one of the evidences they used against him when they were judging the King of kings.

How can you say we should eat your flesh and drink your blood? He was actually referring to his teachings. He was trying to tell them that they should follow his teachings.

That if they sincerely follow his teachings, Satan will not hold them captive. So, his flesh is his teachings, his commandment of, love your God and loves your neighbor;

'Jesus said unto him, Thou shalt love the Lord thy God with all thy heart, and with all thy soul, and with all thy mind. This is the first and great commandment. And the second is like unto it, Thou shalt love thy neighbour as thyself'. (Matthew 22v37-39).

And his blood is his way of life. Reconciliation, Restitution and Restoration. Showing compassion to sinners, the captives, the sick and the poor. In his blood lies the issues of life.

So, when he said that no man comes to the father except through him, he is not blocking anybody from going to God directly, but the fact remains that when you come to God, he will ask you how you managed to come.

No man cometh to the father except through him means that, if you accept him as your personal Lord and savior;

1. You will have visa to heaven
2. You will have right to call God Father at anytime. **Gal 4v6, Rome 8v15**
3. He will convert you from dust to fire.
4. He will give you total freedom from the snare of the fowlers. **Ps. 124v7.**
5. He will make you a fire and you will become a terror to the devil.

For God is Holy. God is so holy that he does not tolerate iniquity. God is so pure that sin irritates him. God has three thrones, that is occupied by the trinity, which are; 1. The throne of Grace, 2. The throne of Mercy 3. The throne of judgment.

The Throne of Grace is occupied by God the father. **Heb.14v16.** The throne of Mercy is occupied by God the Son. **Isa. 16v5.** TheThrone of Judgement is occupied by God the Holy Spirit. **Rev. 20v4.**

When you come to God through Christ, you approach

the throne of Grace and the throne of mercy, when you go to God direct, you approach the throne of judgment and no man can withstand the judgment of God. **James 2v13.**

'Wherefore I say unto you, All manner of sin and blasphemy shall be forgiven unto men: but the blasphemy against the Holy Ghost shall not be forgiven unto men. And whosoever speaketh a word against the Son of man, it shall be forgiven him: but whosoever speaketh against the Holy Ghost, it shall not be forgiven him, neither in this world, neither in the world to come'. (Matt. 12v31-32)

This bible statement is really talking about the judgement of God by third person in the Trinity, which is the Holy Ghost, He does not show mercy to anyone as long as you are judged by him, it must be according to god's law and order. if it is God the father or God the Son, He can tolorete some things because of mercy and grace which he portrays.

The only criteria needed to approach the throne of Grace is to accept Christ as your personal Lord and savior and become converted from dust to fire. So, what makes Christianity different from other religion is the fire.

They say that Christianity is a way of life, that Christianity is not a religion. Christianity minus fire is a religion. In fact, what makes Christianity a way of life is the spirituality in Christianity.

So, Christianity is a religion. It is the spirituality in Christianity that makes it a way of life. In other words, if you minus spirituality from Christianity, it is no more different from other religions.

What makes the spirituality is the presence of fire and the fire is what makes Christianity different from other religions. When there is no fire, Christianity becomes like other religions that hang charms, wear rings and do all manner of rituals for protection and riches.

Where there is fire, there is Holy Ghost, Where there is Holy Ghost, gift of the Holy Ghost is made manifest. Where the gift of the Holy Ghost manifests people are saved from the bondage of the enemies, both internal and external enemies.

Our God gives gift of power to restore his children to their original position from the beginning. He does not give you charm or ring or any other spiritual pantheistic material for power but rather he gives you the gift of the Holy Ghost. **1Corint. 12v8-10**

When you have these gifts, you are bound to succeed in anything you do, because Satan cannot hold you in bondage. It means that you are no more a dust but a fire, you are no more a food to Satan but a terror.

Catch the fire, start burning for Christ and Satan will flee from you. When you become fire, you will start to live a spiritual life like Jesus Christ.

Whenever Christ talks, you hear him referring to his Father in heaven. It shows that he is very conscious of the commandment of his Father in heaven. He is always ready to follow his Father in heaven word-for-word, action-for-action and that is why his Father in heaven calls him Beloved son.

What makes Christianity different is the fire. If you are identified as a Christian and you do not have fire in you, you are not a Christian. Even, from Antioch where the name Christian came from, you will discover that the disciples were burning like fire for Christ, evangelizing, driving out demons, healing the sick, raising the dead and the people around called them Christians; that is, the followers of Christ.

Are you a follower of Christ and you do not have fire in you? You are putting your life in danger. A follower is a disciple that is ready to obey his master word-for-word and action-for-action.

A follower is not a pretender. One day a man from another religion spoke to me; he told me that Christians are not good, they are bad and I asked him how bad. He said in business, they cheat, they are involved in so many immoral activities, they are fraudsters.

I said to him; 'that is the problem'. Those people are not Christians. You cannot be a Christian without fire, and if you are a Christian and you do not have fire, you are merely practicing religion. There is no difference between you and people from other religious sects.

Fire makes the difference. Catch the fire today and burn for Christ today so that you will become a fire and no more a dust.

CHAPTER TWELVE

HOW VIOLENT ARE YOU?

If you know Christ, you will discover that he is not a gentle type when it comes to spiritual issues. Christ looks so gentle in physical appearance but inwardly, he is never gentle. One of the languages Satan understands is violence. You do not plead with him. You do not negotiate with him, rather you exercise your spiritual authority and power over him.

Command the devil, he will flee very far away from you. Beg the devil you will become his meat. One brother was once insane, the family took him to a witch doctor, when they got there, the witch doctor told them to buy so many things (goats, fowls, kolanuts, aligator peppers etc). The parents of the boy agreed to buy those things but because there was no money to buy them, they decided to appease the gods and made pledge to the demon. Instead of getting better, the boy got worst. From slight insanity he became raving mad.

There are two languages Satan understands very well and the two languages are not for gentle people at all;

1. Violence. Satan I rebuke you in the name of Jesus. I command fire from heaven upon you in the name of Jesus. If you are such an individual that exercises these kinds of

spiritual power and authority you will discover that Satan can never come near you and your property.

2. Silence. The best answer to a fool is silence. As a matter of fact, Satan hates it when he is ignored, when he is treated as nobody, when he is treated as a powerless spirit. A man of God was in his house when Satan came to visit him with so many kinds of terrifying noises, the man went and opened the door and it was the devil. The man said to him, 'Oh, Satan are you the one? The man of God never waited for a reply, turned back as if nothing happened. Satan, because he was ignored, felt disgraced, because he was treated as nobody. He became discouraged, because he was treated like an ordinary spirit. He felt ashamed and left.

The bible says that the kingdom of God suffereth violence and the man of violence takes it by force;

"And from the days of John the Baptist until now the kingdom of heaven suffereth violence, and the violent take it by force". (Mt 11:12)

The kingdom of God suffereth violence. This means that the kingdom of darkness is forcefully opposing the advancement of the kingdom of God. In the book of **1Thessalonians 2v8,** Paul was telling the Thessalonians that they wanted to come to them but Satan hindered their coming.

There is a very fierce force opposing the expansion of the kingdom of our God. The kingdom of the dark world is seriously forming alliances against the kingdom of our God. It is either we are aware of it or not, but the fact remains that the battle is very strong and they are determined to wipe off the entire body of Christ from the surface of the earth.

Since the only language the kingdom of darkness

understands is force, so, Christians should apply force to conquer their enemies. Satan uses force against the people of God.

The Kingdom of Darkness forces you to sin against God. They make someone's life miserable and give you condition for joining them or remain miserable.

They enter into our youths today to cause destruction around the town. They possess our young girls and influence them to become half naked so that the righteous will fall.

They are really pushing very hard, forcefully advancing against the kingdom of God.

They have introduced a very deadly device in the so-called church of God; "Come as you are, it doesn't matter, after all God understands" and so on.

They have also destroyed the unity among Christians today. Christianity has become a religion of denomination without central doctrine; each group forms their own doctrine which contradicts others and suits them. Their devices are really working out because they are making the children of God to grow colder than ever.

The violence takes it by force. When someone comes to take what you know very well rightly belongs to you, what will you do?

One thing I am sure of and nobody can convince me in respect of; 'it is God (Jehovah) that created the heaven and the earth'. The world belongs to him. How do I know it? The bible says that;

'For God so love the world that he gave his only begotten son'. (John 3v16).

What did the begotten son come to do? He came to save man from the enemy of God. To redeem man from the hands of the devil so that man will no more become meal for Satan rather a terror to Satan.

God cares for the world, because he is sure that the

world belongs to him. Now, how will a man after building his own house on his own land decides to destroy that house? Do you think anybody who does such is normal?

Satan claims to own the world, but yet determined to destroy the world he claims to own. Can you not see lies beneath his claim?

In the bible, King Solomon delivered a judgment between two women, one lost her son and wanted to claim another person's child. When King Solomon said that he would divide the living child into two, the real mother said no, do not kill the boy, and rather give the child to the other woman because when he grows, he will know his parents. But the second woman said, "Divide the child into two". There is no way you will own something and want to destroy that thing again. **(1King 3v25-26).**

To move the kingdom of God forward, there must be application of force. The time men used to beg Satan is over. You must learn to stand firm on your right. To succeed on the planet earth, you must apply force. Without force, you will go nowhere. Life itself is battle. To leave a peaceful life, you must prepare to face the kingdom of darkness on the battle field.

There is no how you can apply force if the force is not within you. The force is not about physical strength. It is about spiritual strength applied to pull down principalities and powers in high places.

The force can only come if you are a fire. That means that there is fire within you that will generate the force you needed to succeed in life.

There is wickedness going on in the spiritual realm. Peoples' glories are hijacked by the forces of darkness. The glory is used to advance the kingdom of darkness and also given to those that work for them, sadly the rightful owners of the glory find themselves working for the people who had stolen their glory. Abomination!

When a child is born, powers of darkness send their

human agents to come and hijack the glory of the innocent child. The child grows up and begins to suffer and if care is not taken, the child dies.

A woman womb is removed, making her barren. She tries all she could to no avail, because the kingdom of darkness has hijacked her glory.

A man toils around without success because the kingdom of darkness has blocked all his ways, making the man's life miserable.

A person is born blind, lame, deaf and dumb because the kingdom of darkness has done their worst.

People die miserably through accidental, or premature death, brief illness, long sickness and so on. The kingdom of darkness is at work creating pains and sorrows in the life of people.

All these things are evil under the sun. The people of God sit and watch all these and many other evil happen to them. They never make effort to confront the enemy.

Only the violent in the spirit shall take their destiny by force. If you want to be violent in the spiritual realm, you must become fire for Christ.

You must be ready to burn like fire for the kingdom of God. You must burn down all the devices of the evil ones. The kingdom of darkness must see you as a terror.

When Satan sees you as a terror, evil forces will keep away from your children, wife, husband, father, mother, uncles, aunts, siblings, property, friends, and members of your ministry. He will keep away from them because if he dares any of them, fire will destroy him.

The time to take back everything that belongs to you which Satan is holding captive of is now. There is no other way you can practice your Christian faith without fire. You must learn how to take it by force. Become a fire today.

GOD BLESS YOU

Printed in the United States
By Bookmasters